VOL. 12

HAL•LEONARD
UKULELE
PLAY-ALONG

Bluegrass
FAVORITES

Ukulele – Chris Kringel
Mandolin and Banjo – Jon Peik
Guitar – Mike DeRose
Tracking, mixing, and mastering – Chris Kringel and Jake Johnson

ISBN 978-1-4584-1659-9

HAL•LEONARD®
CORPORATION
7777 W. BLUEMOUND RD. P.O. BOX 13819 MILWAUKEE, WI 53213

Visit Hal Leonard Online at
www.halleonard.com

CONTENTS

TRACK 1

Angel Band

Words and Music by Ralph Stanley

Chorus

Oh, come, an - gel band. _____ Come and a - round _____ me _____ stand. Oh, bear me a - way on your snow - white wings _____ to my im - mor - tal home. _____ Oh, bear me a - way on your

1. snow - white wings _____ to my im - mor - tal home.

2. my im - mor - tal home.

rit.

Dooley

Words by Mitchell F. Jayne
Music by Rodney Dillard

TRACK 3

boil - ers, the oth - er watched the spout.
trad - er when in - to town he come,
moun - tain, he lies there all a - lone. They

Ma - ma corked __ the bot - tles and old Doo - ley fetched 'em
sug - ar by ____ the bush - el and mo - las - ses by the
put a jug ____ be - side him and a bar - rel for a

Chorus

out. Doo - ley, slip - pin' up a hol - ler.
ton.
stone.

Doo - ley, try'n' to make a dol - lar. Doo - ley,

give me a swal - ler and I'll pay you back __ some - day.

1., 2.   3.

And I'll pay you back __ some - day.

7

Fox on the Run

Words and Music by Tony Hazzard

TRACK 5

First note

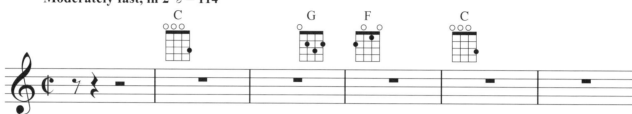

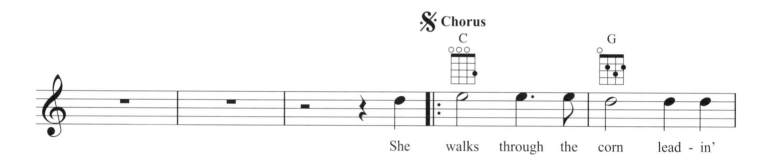

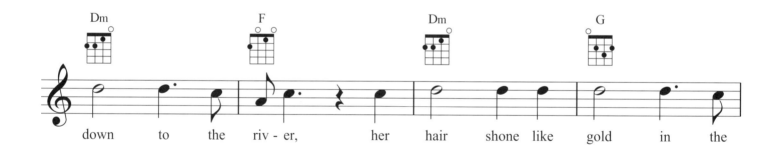

She walks through the corn lead-in'
down to the riv-er, her hair shone like gold in the

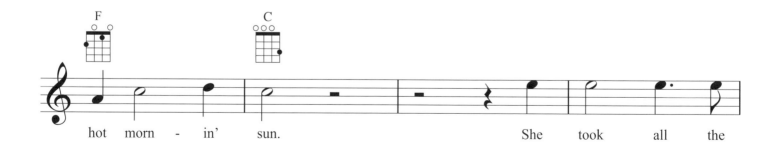

hot morn-in' sun.   She took all the

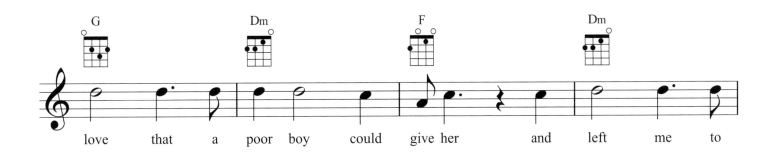

love   that   a   poor   boy   could   give   her   and   left   me   to

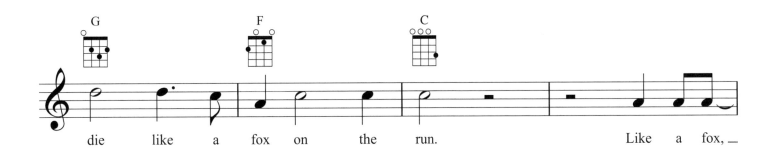

die   like   a   fox   on   the   run.   Like   a   fox, __

____   like   a   fox, ____   like   a   fox, ____   like   a   fox __

To Coda

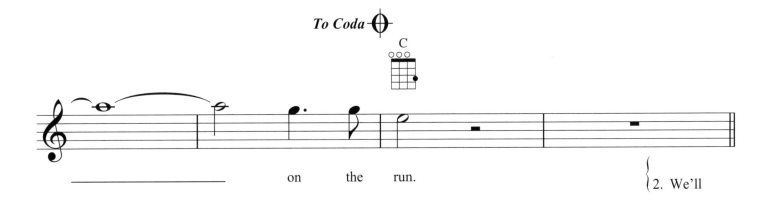

_____   on   the   run.   2. We'll

Verse

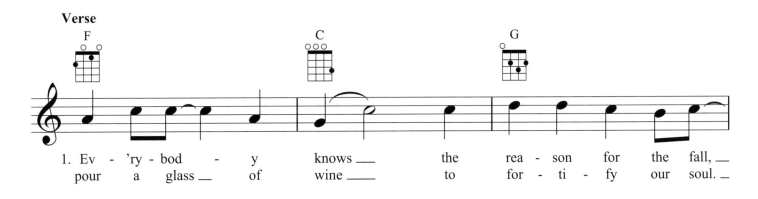

1. Ev - 'ry - bod - y   knows __   the   rea - son   for   the   fall, __

pour   a   glass __   of   wine __   to   for - ti - fy   our   soul. __

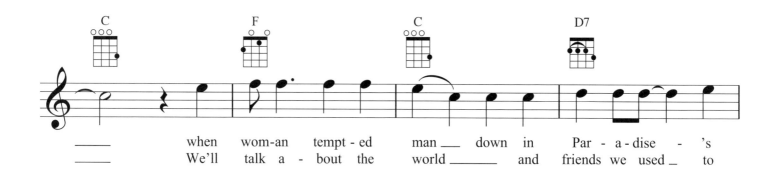

_____ when wom-an tempt-ed man ___ down in Par-a-dise -'s
_____ We'll talk a - bout the world _____ and friends we used _ to

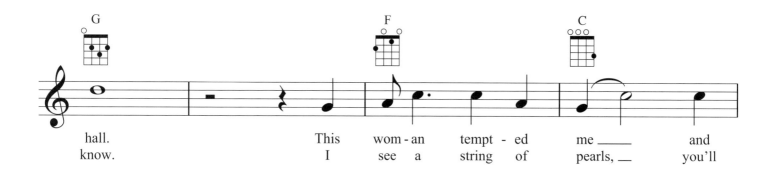

hall. This wom-an tempt-ed me _____ and
know. I see a string of pearls, __ you'll

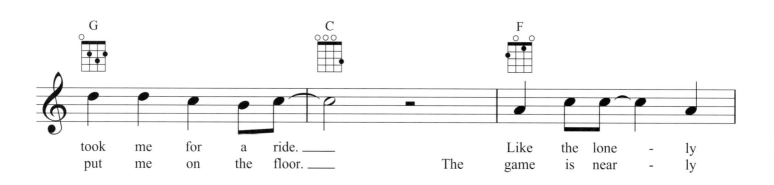

took me for a ride. _____ The Like the lone - ly
put me on the floor. _____ The Like game is near - ly

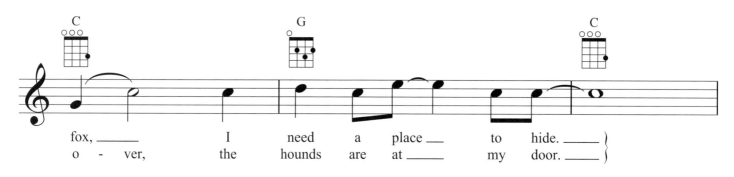

fox, _____ I need a place __ to hide. _____ }
o - ver, the hounds are at _____ my door. _____ }

2nd time, D.S. al Coda

⊕ **Coda**

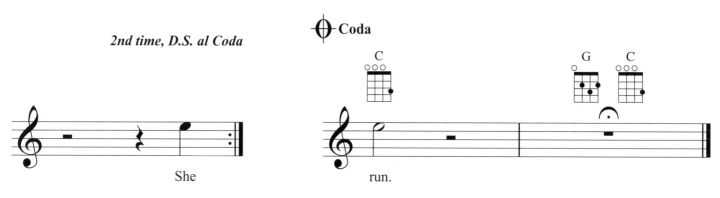

She

run.

I Am a Man of Constant Sorrow

Words and Music by Carter Stanley

TRACK 7

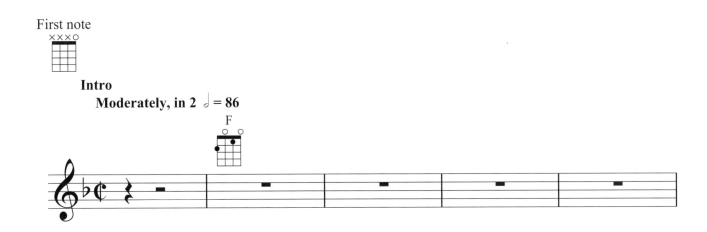

First note

Intro
Moderately, in 2 ♩ = 86

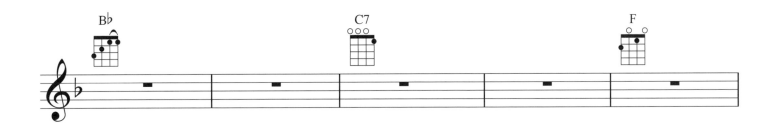

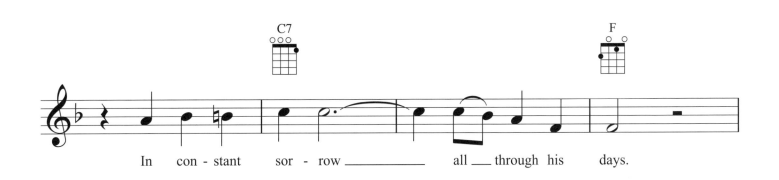

In con - stant sor - row _____ all __ through his days.

Verse

1. I _____ am the man _____
2. For _____ six long years _____
3. It's _____ fare thee well, _____
4., 5. *See additional lyrics*

_____ of con - stant sor - row, _____ I've __ seen trou -
_____ I've been __ in trou - ble, _____ no plea - sure here __
_____ my old __ true lov - er. _____ I nev - er ex - pect __

- _____ ble all __ my days. I _____
_____ on earth __ I find. For _____
_____ to see you a - gain. For _____

_____ bid fare - well _____ to old __ Ken -
_____ in this world _____ I'm bound __ to
_____ I'm bound to ride _____ that North - ern

tuck - y, _____ the place __ where I _____
ram - ble, _____ I have __ no friends _____
rail - road; _____ per - haps __ I'll die _____

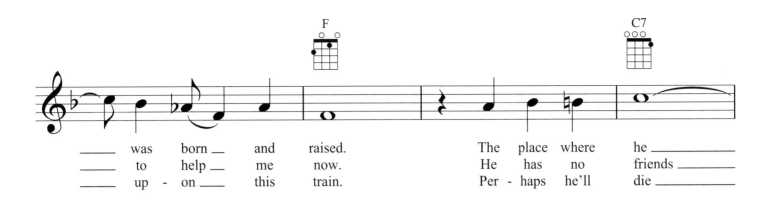

_____ was born _____ and raised.
_____ to help _____ me now.
_____ up - on _____ this train.

The place where he _____
He has no friends _____
Per - haps he'll die _____

1. - 4.   **Guitar Solo/Interlude**

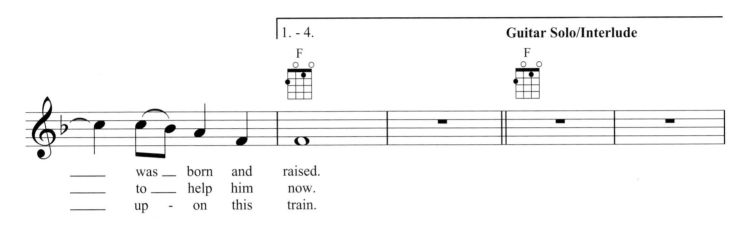

_____ was _____ born and raised.
_____ to _____ help him now.
_____ up - on this train.

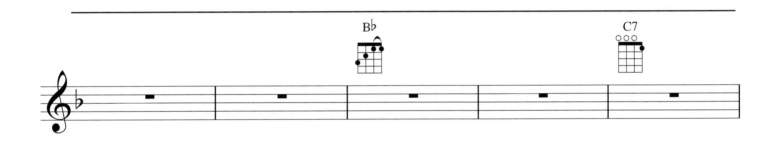

5.

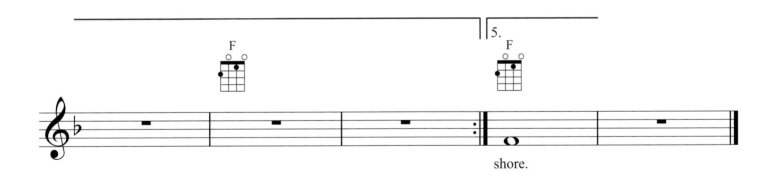

shore.

Additional Lyrics

4. You can bury me in some deep valley,
   For many years where I may lay.
   And you may learn to love another
   While I am sleeping in my grave.
   While he is sleeping in his grave.

5. Maybe your friends think I'm just a stranger.
   My face you never will see no more.
   But there is one promise that is given,
   I'll meet you on God's golden shore.
   He'll meet you on God's golden shore.

TRACK 9

I'll Fly Away

Words and Music by Albert E. Brumley

First note

Intro
Moderately, in 2 ♩ = 100

Verse

1. Some bright morn - ing when this life is
2. When the sha - dows of this life have
3. Oh, how glad and hap - py when we
4. Just a few more wear - y days and

o'er,
gone,
meet,
then,

I'll _____ fly a - way,

to that home on God's ce - les - tial shore,
like a bird from these pri - son walls I'll fly,
no more cold darn shack - les on my feet,
to a land where joys will nev - er end,

I'll _____

Chorus

_____ fly a - way. I'll _____ fly a -

way, oh glo - ry, I'll _____ fly a - way in the

morn - ing. When I die Hal - le - lu - ia by and by,

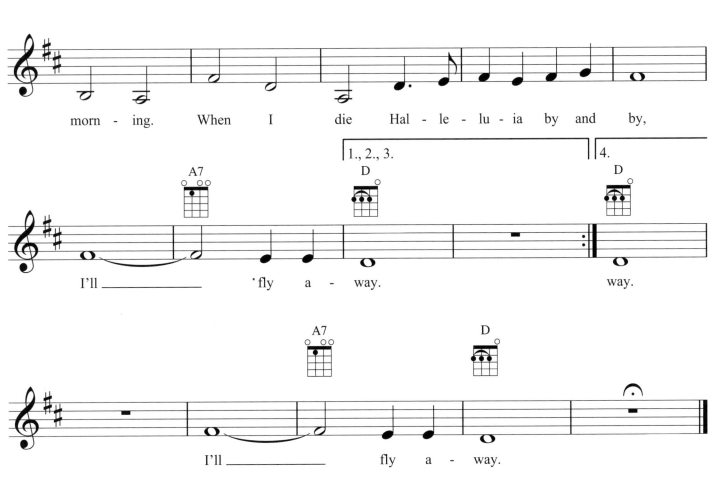

1., 2., 3.

I'll _____ 'fly a - way.

4.

way.

I'll _____ fly a - way.

Keep on the Sunny Side

Words and Music by A.P. Carter

Sitting on Top of the World

Words and Music by Walter Jacobs and Lonnie Carter

TRACK 13

First note

Intro
Moderately fast, in 2 ♩ = 150

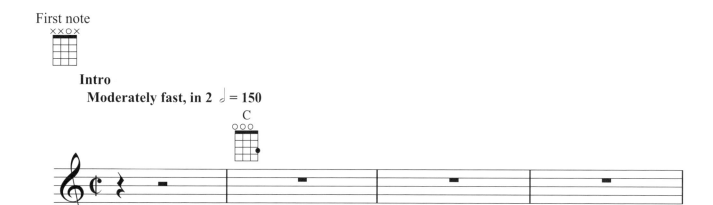

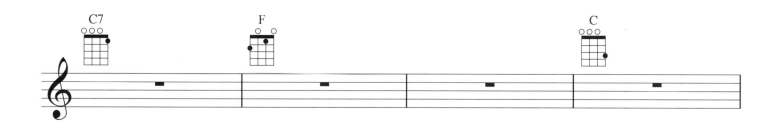

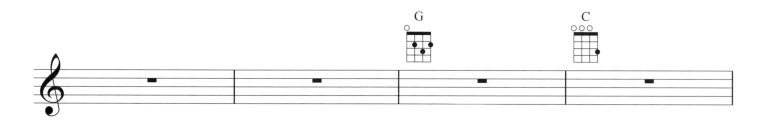

18

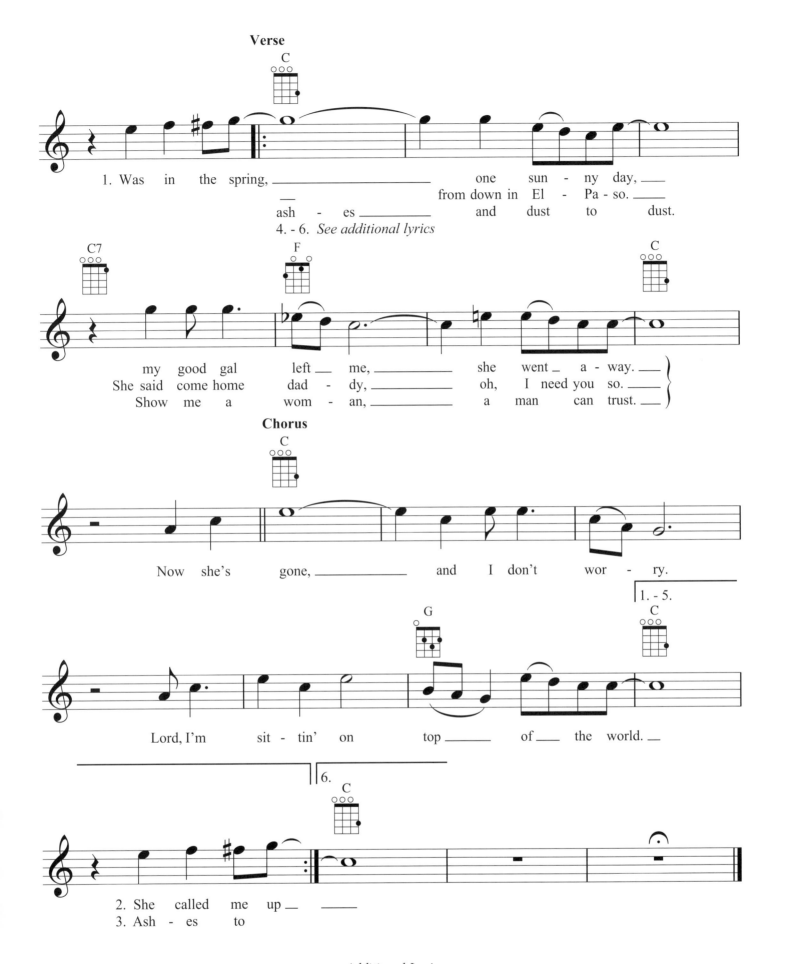

Verse

1. Was in the spring, _____ one sun - ny day, ____
    _____ from down in El - Pa - so. ____
ash - es _____ and dust to dust.

4. - 6. *See additional lyrics*

my good gal left __ me, _____ she went __ a - way. ____
She said come home dad - dy, _____ oh, I need you so. ____
Show me a wom - an, _____ a man can trust. ____

Chorus

Now she's gone, _____ and I don't wor - ry.

1. - 5.

Lord, I'm sit - tin' on top _____ of __ the world. __

6.

2. She called me up __ ____
3. Ash - es to

Additional Lyrics

4. Mississippi River
   Runs deep and wide.
   The gal I'm loving
   Is on the other side.

5. If you don't like my peaches,
   Don't you shake my tree.
   Stay out of my orchard
   And let the peaches be.

6. Don't come to me
   Holding out your hand.
   I'll just get me a woman
   Just like you got your man.

With Body and Soul

Words and Music by Virginia Stauffer

TRACK 15

First note

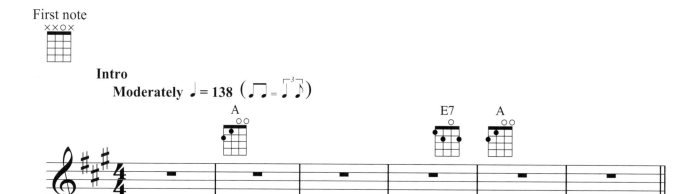

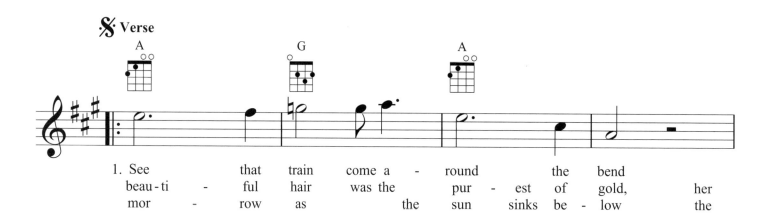

1. See that train come a - round the bend the
beau - ti - ful train hair was the pur - est of gold, her
mor - row as the sun sinks be - low her

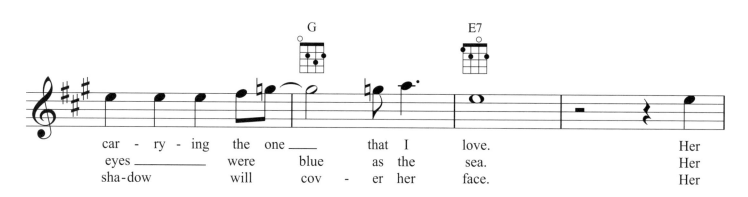

car - ry - ing the one ___ that I love. Her
eyes ___ were blue as the sea. Her
sha - dow will cov - er her face. Her

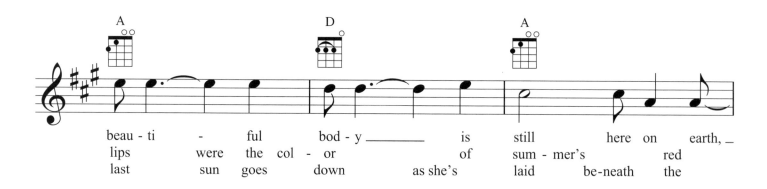

beau - ti - ful bod - y ___ is still here on earth, ___
lips were the col - or of sum - mer's red
last sun goes down as she's laid be - neath the

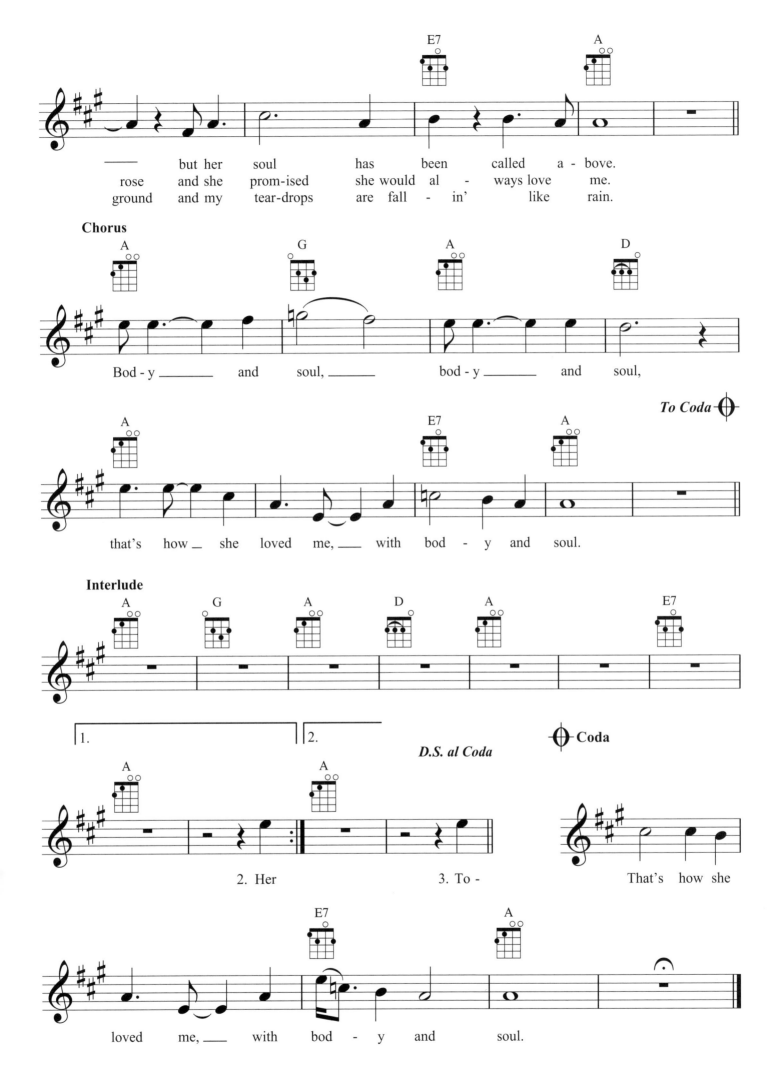

but her soul has been called a - bove.
rose and she prom-ised she would al - ways love me.
ground and my tear-drops are fall - in' like rain.

Chorus

Bod - y _____ and soul, _____ bod - y _____ and soul,

that's how ___ she loved me, ___ with bod - y and soul.

Interlude

1. 2.

D.S. al Coda

Coda

2. Her 3. To - That's how she

loved me, ___ with bod - y and soul.

HAL·LEONARD UKULELE PLAY-ALONG®

> *Now you can play your favorite songs on your uke with great-sounding backing tracks to help you sound like a bona fide pro!*

1. POP HITS
American Pie • Copacabana (At the Copa) • Crocodile Rock • Kokomo • Lean on Me • Stand by Me • Twist and Shout • What the World Needs Now Is Love.
00701451 Book/CD Pack.............$14.99

2. UKE CLASSICS
Ain't She Sweet • Five Foot Two, Eyes of Blue (Has Anybody Seen My Girl?) • It's Only a Paper Moon • Living in the Sunlight, Loving in the Moonlight • Pennies from Heaven • Tonight You Belong to Me • Ukulele Lady • When I'm Cleaning Windows.
00701452 Book/CD Pack.............$12.99

3. HAWAIIAN FAVORITES
Aloha Oe • Blue Hawaii • Harbor Lights • The Hawaiian Wedding Song (Ke Kali Nei Au) • Mele Kalikimaka • Sleepy Lagoon • Sweet Someone • Tiny Bubbles.
00701453 Book/CD Pack.............$12.99

4. CHILDREN'S SONGS
Do-Re-Mi • The Hokey Pokey • It's a Small World • My Favorite Things • Puff the Magic Dragon • Sesame Street Theme • Splish Splash • This Land Is Your Land.
00701454 Book/CD Pack.............$12.99

5. CHRISTMAS SONGS
INCLUDES TAB
Do You Hear What I Hear • Feliz Navidad • Frosty the Snow Man • Here Comes Santa Claus (Right down Santa Claus Lane) • Jingle-Bell Rock • Nuttin' for Christmas • Rudolph the Red-Nosed Reindeer • Santa Claus Is Comin' to Town.
00701696 Book/CD Pack.............$12.99

6. LENNON & McCARTNEY
And I Love Her • Day Tripper • Here, There and Everywhere • Hey Jude • Let It Be • Norwegian Wood (This Bird Has Flown) • Nowhere Man • Yesterday.
00701723 Book/CD Pack.............$12.99

7. DISNEY FAVORITES
Alice in Wonderland • The Bare Necessities • Candle on the Water • Chim Chim Cher-ee • A Dream Is a Wish Your Heart Makes • Mickey Mouse March • Supercalifragilisticexpialidocious • Under the Sea.
00701724 Book/CD Pack.............$12.99

8. CHART HITS
All the Right Moves • Bubbly • Hey, Soul Sister • I'm Yours • Toes • Use Somebody • Viva la Vida • You're Beautiful.
00701745 Book/CD Pack.............$12.99

9. THE SOUND OF MUSIC
Climb Ev'ry Mountain • Do-Re-Mi • Edelweiss • Maria • My Favorite Things • Sixteen Going on Seventeen • Something Good • The Sound of Music.
00701784 Book/CD Pack.............$12.99

11. CHRISTMAS STRUMMING
Away in a Manger • Deck the Hall • The First Noel • Hark! the Herald Angels Sing • Jingle Bells • Joy to the World • O Come, All Ye Faithful (Adeste Fideles) • We Three Kings of Orient Are.
00702458 Book/CD Pack.............$12.99

13. UKULELE SONGS
Daughter • Dream a Little Dream of Me • Elderly Woman Behind the Counter in a Small Town • Last Kiss • More Than You Know • Sleepless Nights • Tonight You Belong to Me • Yellow Ledbetter.
00702599 Book/CD Pack.............$12.99

FOR MORE INFORMATION, SEE YOUR LOCAL MUSIC DEALER, OR WRITE TO:

HAL·LEONARD® CORPORATION
7777 W. BLUEMOUND RD. P.O. BOX 13819 MILWAUKEE, WI 53213

www.halleonard.com

Prices, contents, and availability subject to change without notice.
Disney characters and artwork © Disney Enterprises, Inc.

1111

Learn to play the
Ukulele
with these great Hal Leonard books!

Hal Leonard Ukulele Method Book 1
by Lil' Rev

The *Hal Leonard Ukulele Method* is designed for anyone just learning to play ukulele. This comprehensive and easy-to-use beginner's guide by acclaimed performer and uke master Lil' Rev includes many fun songs of different styles to learn and play. The accompanying CD contains 46 tracks of songs for demonstration and play along. Includes: types of ukuleles, tuning, music reading, melody playing, chords, strumming, scales, tremolo, music notation and tablature, a variety of music styles, ukulele history and much more.

00695847 Book Only.. $5.99
00695832 Book/CD Pack $10.99
00320534 DVD $14.95

Hal Leonard Ukulele Method Book 2
by Lil' Rev

Book 2 picks up where Book 1 left off, featuring more fun songs and examples to strengthen skills and make practicing more enjoyable. Topics include lessons on chord families, hammer-ons, pull-offs, and slides, 6/8 time, ukulele history, and much more. The accompanying CD contains 51 tracks of songs for demonstration and play along.

00695948 Book Only.. $5.95
00695949 Book/CD Pack $9.95

Hal Leonard Ukulele Chord Finder
Easy-to-Use Guide to Over 1,000 Ukulele Chords

Learn to play chords on the ukulele with this comprehensive, yet easy-to-use book. *The Ukulele Chord Finder* contains more than a thousand chord diagrams for the most important 28 chord types, including three voicings for each chord. Also includes a lesson on chord construction and a fingerboard chart of the ukulele neck!

00695803 9" x 12".. $6.95
00695902 6" x 9"... $4.99

Hal Leonard Ukulele Scale Finder
by Chad Johnson
Easy-to-Use Guide to Over 1,300 Ukulele Scales

Learn to play scales on the ukulele with this comprehensive yet easy-to-use book. *The Ukulele Scale Finder* contains over 1,300 scale diagrams for the most often-used scales and modes, including multiple patterns for each scale. Also includes a lesson on scale construction and a fingerboard chart of the ukulele neck!

00696378 9" x 12".. $6.99

Easy Songs for Ukulele
Play the Melodies of 20 Pop, Folk, Country, and Blues Songs
by Lil' Rev

Play along with your favorite tunes from the Beatles, Elvis, Johnny Cash, Woody Guthrie, Simon & Garfunkel, and more! The songs are presented in the order of difficulty, beginning with simple rhythms and melodies and ending with chords and notes up the neck. The audio CD features every song played with guitar accompaniment, so you can hear how each song sounds and then play along when you're ready.

00695904 Book/CD Pack $14.99
00695905 Book $6.99

Irving Berlin Songs Arranged for the "Uke"

20 great songs with full instructions, including: Alexander's Ragtime Band • White Christmas • Easter Parade • Say It with Music • and more.

00005558 7" x 10-1/4" $6.95

Fretboard Roadmaps – Ukulele
The Essential Patterns That All the Pros Know and Use
by Fred Sokolow & Jim Beloff

Take your uke playing to the next level! Tunes and exercises in standard notation and tab illustrate each technique. Absolute beginners can follow the diagrams and instruction step-by-step, while intermediate and advanced players can use the chapters non-sequentially to increase their understanding of the ukulele. The CD includes 59 demo and play-along tracks.

00695901 Book/CD Pack... $14.99

Play Ukulele Today!
A Complete Guide to the Basics
by Barrett Tagliarino

This is the ultimate self-teaching method for ukulele! Includes a CD with full demo tracks and over 60 great songs. You'll learn: care for the instrument; how to produce sound; reading music notation and rhythms; and more.

00699638 Book/CD Pack.. $9.99

www.halleonard.com

Prices, contents and availability subject to change without notice. Prices listed in U.S. funds.

HAL•LEONARD® CORPORATION
7777 W. BLUEMOUND RD. P.O. BOX 13819
MILWAUKEE, WISCONSIN 53213

0911

Ride the Ukulele Wave!

The Beach Boys for Ukulele

This folio features 20 favorites, including: Barbara Ann • Be True to Your School • California Girls • Fun, Fun, Fun • God Only Knows • Good Vibrations • Help Me Rhonda • I Get Around • In My Room • Kokomo • Little Deuce Coupe • Sloop John B • Surfin' U.S.A. • Wouldn't It Be Nice • and more.

00701726 . . . . $14.99

Disney Songs for Ukulele

20 great Disney classics arranged for all uke players, including: Beauty and the Beast • Bibbidi-Bobbidi-Boo (The Magic Song) • Can You Feel the Love Tonight • Chim Chim Cher-ee • Heigh-Ho • It's a Small World • Some Day My Prince Will Come • We're All in This Together • When You Wish upon a Star • and more.

00701708 . . . . $12.99

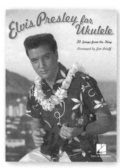

Elvis Presley for Ukulele

arr. Jim Beloff

20 classic hits from The King: All Shook Up • Blue Hawaii • Blue Suede Shoes • Can't Help Falling in Love • Don't • Heartbreak Hotel • Hound Dog • Jailhouse Rock • Love Me • Love Me Tender • Return to Sender • Suspicious Minds • Teddy Bear • and more.

00701004 . . . . $14.99

The Beatles for Ukulele

Ukulele players can strum, sing and pick along with 20 Beatles classics! Includes: All You Need Is Love • Eight Days a Week • Good Day Sunshine • Here, There and Everywhere • Let It Be • Love Me Do • Penny Lane • Yesterday • and more.

00700154 . . . . $16.99

Folk Songs for Ukulele

A great collection to take along to the campfire! 60 folk songs, including: Amazing Grace • Buffalo Gals • Camptown Races • For He's a Jolly Good Fellow • Good Night Ladies • Home on the Range • I've Been Working on the Railroad • Kumbaya • My Bonnie Lies over the Ocean • On Top of Old Smoky • Scarborough Fair • Swing Low, Sweet Chariot • Take Me Out to the Ball Game • Yankee Doodle • and more.

00696068 . . . . $12.99

Hawaiian Songs for Ukulele

Over thirty songs from the state that made the ukulele famous, including: Beyond the Rainbow • Hanalei Moon • Ka-lu-a • Lovely Hula Girl • Mele Kalikimaka • One More Aloha • Sea Breeze • Tiny Bubbles • Waikiki • and more.

00696065 . . . . $9.99

Irving Berlin Songs Arranged for the "Uke"

20 great songs with full instructions, including: Always • Blue Skies • Easter Parade • How Deep Is the Ocean (How High Is the Sky) • A Pretty Girl Is like a Melody • Say It with Music • What'll I Do? • White Christmas • and more.

00005558 . . . . $6.95

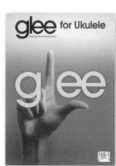

Glee

Music from the Fox Television Show for Ukulele

20 favorites for Gleeks to strum and sing, including: Bad Romance • Beautiful • Defying Gravity • Don't Stop Believin' • No Air • Proud Mary • Rehab • True Colors • and more.

00701722 . . . $14.99

Worship Songs for Ukulele

25 worship songs: Amazing Grace (My Chains are Gone) • Blessed Be Your Name • Enough • God of Wonders • Holy Is the Lord • How Great Is Our God • In Christ Alone • Love the Lord • Mighty to Save • Sing to the King • Step by Step • We Fall Down • and more.

00702546 . . . . $12.99

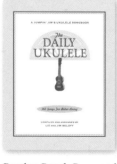

The Daily Ukulele

compiled and arranged by Liz and Jim Beloff

Strum a different song everyday with easy arrangements of 365 of your favorite songs in one big songbook! Includes favorites by the Beatles, Beach Boys, and Bob Dylan, folk songs, pop songs, kids' songs, Christmas carols, and Broadway and Hollywood tunes, all with a spiral binding for ease of use.

00240356 . . . . $34.99

Jake Shimabukuro – Peace Love Ukulele

Deemed "the Hendrix of the ukulele," Hawaii native Jake Shimabukuro is a uke virtuoso. Our songbook features note-for-note transcriptions with ukulele tablature of Jake's masterful playing on all the CD tracks: Bohemian Rhapsody • Boy Meets Girl • Bring Your Adz • Hallelujah • Pianoforte 2010 • Variation on a Dance 2010 • and more, plus two bonus selections!

00702516 . . . . $19.99

Rodgers & Hammerstein for Ukulele

arr. Jim Beloff

Now you can play 20 classic show tunes from this beloved songwriting duo on your uke! Includes: All at Once You Love Her • Do-Re-Mi • Edelweiss • Getting to Know You • Impossible • My Favorite Things • and more.

00701905 . . . . $12.99

Disney characters and artwork © Disney Enterprises, Inc.

Prices, contents, and availability subject to change.

HAL•LEONARD® CORPORATION
7777 W. BLUEMOUND RD. P.O. BOX 13819 MILWAUKEE, WI 53213

0212